For my Dad.

A.E.Delman, PhD

Money
Plain & Simple

Change your Money Role.
Change your life.

penny pincher

underachiever

pious

martyr

reckless

uncertain

deal chaser

unfulfilled

Money
Plain & Simple™

Acknowledgments

First of all I owe special thanks to **Monica Goyal**, my business partner, who has helped me create this book, contributed critical advice and is endlessly patient, supportive and insightful. Monica knows this material and like me lives its principles. Thanks to Monica there will be more books and programs to come.

Thanks to **Jennifer Christmas** for reading, editing, contributing ideas, for the countless long telephone conversation about Money Roles and for being an essential member of the team. Thanks, Jen for your unwavering faith.

I would like to thank **Nick Piquard** for his support, time and his many contributions.

Thanks to **Rich McLay** for his writing contributions, for helping me clarify my ideas and for the great deal of care he brought to this project.

Thanks to **Kamilla Nikolaev** and **Joshua Emberlin** for their excellent book design.

I am also grateful to **Jason Cheong-Kee** -You who has been an enthusiastic promoter of my work and who has always generously shared his network, ideas and solutions.

I would like to thank **Tom Schur** for many good discussions about self and systems, for his encouragement and for sharing his experience and ideas.

Thanks also to my Syracuse, NY network of friends for their support.

My deep appreciation goes to the members of my "money and family" groups who helped me formulate this program. Thanks also to the Toronto genogram group.

Thanks to **Joan Sohn** and **Charlene Richards** for patiently educating Monica and I about book design and printing. Thanks Joan for acting as the design advisor and for your support.

Thanks to my friends who let me pick their brains, who read and edited and who cheered me through this process.

Thanks to my family who has given me continual support and love in all that I have done. I owe you a heartfelt thank you.

And most importantly, thanks to my mother and father for being present and for inspiring me.

Change your

Money Role

Change your

life

Welcome

to Money Plain & Simple.™ My name is Dr. Aimee Delman. I work and advise in Human Social Development. I've helped women, men, couples, individuals, executives and employees come to grips with the way they relate to money. I counsel people who struggle to pay the rent on time, the ultra-rich, and everyone in between.

Over the years, I've learned that there are two absolutes:

1 Money issues are never ultimately about money, and
2 Intelligent, capable people from all walks of life have money issues. Nobody is immune.

If you're like most people, you know what you'd like to achieve, the challenge is how to get there. Money Plain & Simple provides a foolproof map to reaching your goals by addressing the root of your financial decision making: your Money Role. I've carefully designed the Money Plain & Simple program to give you the skills, insight and awareness you need to understand and change your relationship with money. Because when you change your Money Role, you change your life.

Money Plain & Simple Works for Everybody

Money Plain & Simple is a powerful, easy-to-follow program that can help anyone get to the bottom of their financial challenges.

Have you ever wondered:
• Why am I accomplishing and earning less than my potential?
• Why is it so difficult to get out of debt?
• Why do relationships with loved ones often suffer when there's money involved?
• Why don't I have better common sense about money decisions?

It's a tool for life

Money Plain & Simple provides answers to questions like these and gives you the personalized tools you need to achieve lasting financial security and success.

It's Easy

Money Plain & Simple requires no financial know-how and is perfect for anyone who's overwhelmed by money issues. You won't need a calculator, or accounting software; you won't have to create a budget, or pore over your bank account statements. Money Plain & Simple isn't about numbers, it's about you.

I've used my experience to design a program that helps you realize how you really relate to money. Using Money Plain & Simple you'll delve into your habits, decision making, and planning to discover what makes you tick. You'll build the confidence to take control over the forces and relationships that shape your financial life.

Money Plain & Simple is three products in one – a powerful financial solution, an easy-to-follow three step program, and a long-term financial planning tool. It answers your financial questions and gives you personalized solutions, strategies and a Logbook with tools to plan and chart your progress.

How do I use Money Plain & Simple?

Money Plain & Simple provides you with a flexible, easy-to-follow program that allows you to proceed at your own pace. As you advance through the Money Plain & Simple program you'll be selecting your Money Focus, getting on top of your Money Role and understanding your Money Habits by following Three Simple Steps:

1 Creating Smart Habits to change your relationship with money
2 Mastering Smart Decisions with a new approach to Financial Decisions
3 Using Smart Strategies to Plan for Success

All of these changes will drastically improve your relationship with money. Your Money Role will feel different, changed for the better and you will have the tools and understanding to achieve your financial goals.

Let's get started

Over the years I have seen all kinds of money problems. I have worked with families torn apart by money conflicts, capable people paralyzed by money decisions, parents undermining their children's independence, employees sabotaging their financial advancement and couples using money as a form of control. I wrote Money Plain & Simple because I wanted to explain how smart, hardworking people could make irrational and costly financial decisions. The program provides solutions for all kinds of challenges and works for all types of people, myself included. Money Plain & Simple comes from my work and everything in the program, its principles, steps and strategies is based on the way I live my life.

If you're ready to totally change the way you relate to money and take control of your financial future, then let's get started.

1 Review and complete the section entitled, *Getting Started*.
2 Read the book. It's short, and along the way you'll pick up expert tips and strategies that will prepare you for success.
3 Return to *Three Simple Steps* and begin.

YOUR PERSONAL NAVIGATOR

Money Plain & Simple is a personal program, but you're not entirely alone. From time to time you'll see a box like this one, in which I provide advice and strategy. For additional information and support, I invite you to visit:
www.moneyplainandsimple.com

Table of Contents

Getting

started

What's **your** Money Role?

Money Plain & Simple: Getting Started

What's a Money Role?

Everyone has a particular emotional response to money. I call these responses Money Roles. There are eight Money Roles; each with a distinct approach to spending, saving, providing and earning.

The key to your financial success is your Money Role. Your Money Role is the powerful drive that influences how you think and feel about money. Money Roles are behind all our decisions and they define our financial beliefs and habits. Money Roles wield a lot of power over our lives and can override our own best interests without us realizing it.

Money Plain & Simple helps you take control of your Money Role. Understanding how your Money Role directs your life is the key to changing your relationship with money and achieving your goals.

Everybody has one

Money Roles are a part of life, everybody has one. Money Roles are shaped by our upbringing, family and major life experiences, but when you get right down to it, they're made up of emotions. A Money Role comes from the feelings of comfort, fear and concern we've learned to associate with money.

Is my Money Role good or bad?

Money Roles by themselves aren't good or bad, and no Money Role is better than another. After all, what's wrong with saving money? What's wrong with spending it? The real problem is the degree to which your Money Role dictates your behavior. Spending or saving becomes a problem only if it paralyzes you from doing what is good for yourself. Even when our Money Roles are not paralyzing us, they are always there directing every financial choice we make and preventing us from meeting our real needs.

Control your role

No matter how big or small, situations that involve money trigger concerns and fears and bring out our Money Role. The key to sound financial decisions is learning to recognize how your Money Role directs your decisions. Money Plain & Simple teaches you to see the relationship between your Money Role and the things you do and shows you how to take control of your Money Role. The Money Plain & Simple program is a proven method for putting you back in the financial driver's seat.

Can I really change my Money Role?

Imagine your Money Role is a car. You can install new shocks, tires and brake pads. You can change the oil, have a sunroof put in, and buy a new stereo. All of these changes improve your driving experience. Your car is now different, it's changed for the better, but it's still fundamentally your car. Your Money Role is the same.

What if I pick the wrong Money Role?

Money Plain & Simple is a program that helps you develop a better understanding of how you relate to money. As you begin to pay closer attention to your Money Habits and behaviors, you may decide that your primary Money Role is different than you first thought. That's okay. Rethinking your primary Money Role is normal and means you're making progress.

Money Roles

These definitions are approximate. Choose the best fit.

Your Money Role is emotional and irrational.	**Martyr**	*I can't consider saying no to my kids. When they ask me for money, I just say yes.*
Your Money Role pushes you in one direction, narrowing your options and perspective.	**Underachiever**	*I won't apply for the promotion, I doubt I am qualified. I am going to be poor forever.*
There is a constant tension between your Money Role habits and your financial well-being.	**Reckless**	*I always treat myself to nice things. Life is short and I deserve some rewards.*

My Money Role is:

UNCERTAIN

As a child you were sheltered from financial realities. As a result, you tend to be unsure about money decisions, managing your finances, and achieving your career and financial goals. You look for people to help you manage your money so you don't have to. You don't follow a financial plan. You put off dealing with expenses, taxes, loans and investments. You're hard working and motivated.

My Money Role is:

RECKLESS

Shopping makes you feel better. It makes you feel energized, even gives you a high. Sales are hard to ignore. You spend to celebrate, to deal with stress, when you're angry, when you're having problems, if you're bored, or when you're dealing with change. Your spending has created tension in at least one of your major relationships. You sometimes hide or lie about purchases. You often buy regardless of affordability and need. You justify your purchases by rationalizing it or inventing a need.

My Money Role is:

PENNY PINCHER

You hate spending money unless it's a business investment. You can be frugal and cheap. Your goal is wealth and your career occupies most of your attention. You closely monitor your savings. You tend to obsess about financial decisions. You judge your friends and family's Money Habits and lecture or fight with them about their behavior. You're always worried about having enough money, regardless of how much you earn. You believe money is the only true form of security.

My Money Role is:

DEAL CHASER

You see the next big deal as your financial solution. You think the next big deal will make you rich, secure, happy and successful. Getting rich quick will fix any problems you have with family and friends. You've neglected your paid work for the big deal. You've risked your savings, your job, and your friendships in pursuit of the big deal. It's hard for you to listen to criticism about your big deal. You believe your lucky break is going to be sudden and huge.

My Money Role is:

UNDERACHIEVER

Your lack of confidence in yourself and your own abilities is unfair. Because you don't fully appreciate your strengths and capabilities, you underestimate yourself. As a result you take work below your full potential. You have a hard time asking for a raise, seeking promotion and investing in yourself. Financial opportunities and decisions are intimidating. Sometimes you avoid them because you think they're beyond your control. You wait for others to make decisions. You are cautious and conservative around money. You constantly worry that you'll make poor financial choices and you will not be able to meet your obligations.

My Money Role is:
PIOUS

You see the pursuit of money and material wealth as somehow misguided, even unethical. You're proud of the fact your lifestyle isn't consumed by money and materialism. Sometimes you may even feel slightly self-righteous. You lead a simple, frugal life because you have a shortage of money. You insist money isn't your priority, but your lack of money is often a problem. You can be generous to charities.

My Money Role is:

UNFULFILLED

You don't really enjoy what you do for a living, and your job may even conflict with your values, but you do it because the money is convenient. You're willing to sacrifice for others but rarely do so for yourself. You tend to put off investing time or money in any kind of major self-improvement project. Sometimes you wonder what you might have done had you made different choices. Both your work and personal life do not demand that you use your full range of creative or intellectual skills. You are successful, responsible and pragmatic.

My Money Role is:

MARTYR

People in your life look to you for money because you're generous. You willingly take on more than your fair share of financial responsibility. You give money, advice and guidance to people whose poor Money Habits leave them living beyond their means. You have a hard time saying no to requests for money because you believe that those you help will suffer without your support and guidance. You keep funds available so you can provide last minute financial help.

Make Decisions
Get out of Debt
Be independent
End financial
self-sabotage
Deal with
Relationships
Get ahead

Before you start the Money Plain & Simple program you need to answers these three key questions.

1 What's your focus?

Choose an aspect of your life that involves money, and needs to change. It may involve a personal relationship, employment, your unfulfilled potential or your family life. Record your answer in the *Logbook* under My Focus.

Now imagine it's the future, you've used Money Plain & Simple to achieve your Focus. Pick one or two things in your life that have improved and write them in the *Logbook* under Improvements.

Steve's Focus:
A good job with a good salary.
Steve's future Improvements:
I have health insurance and I can afford a vacation

Money Plain & Simple is a tool for life. Once you've reached the objectives you're setting now, you'll be able to continue using the program and setting a new Focus and goals.

2 What's your Money Role?

Read through the Money Role descriptions on pages 23–30 while you think about your Focus. To find your Money Role ask yourself what Money Role you play in your relationships, especially those related to your Focus. Look for the big patterns. (Are you the Reckless, the Penny Pincher, the Deal Chaser?) Don't look to others to determine your Money Role. You alone know what really motivates the choices you make with your money.

Most people are a mix of one primary Money Role and two or more minor roles. Choose your primary Money Role. Write your answers in the *Logbook* under My Money Roles and My Primary Money Role.

* Remember your Money Role is not the same as your position in your family (wage earner) or what you do for work (crew manager).

3 What are your Money Habits?

When we fall into our Money Role we repeat certain routine behaviors. These behaviors are Money Habits. Money Habits make us feel good in the short term but work against us in the long term. They're routine, comfortable, and easy to repeat. But we can't ignore them, because Money Habits strengthen our Money Role and keep us from making good choices. Our Money Habits keep us in our financial ruts.

Imagine your Money Role as your company. Money Habits are the underperforming employees that are hurting your bottom line. You need to root out their poor performance and replace them with candidates that will help grow your company instead of shrink it.

Money Plain & Simple will show you how to tap into your Money Role and make positive changes by reshaping your Money Habits into Smart Habits.

Hanah has a lucrative career; she's ambitious and believes saving money is important. She's also the main provider in her household. Hanah enjoys shopping and thinking about things she'd like to buy. Buying is her outlet for stress, boredom and for celebrating. When her kids ask for something they usually get it. She has a hard time saying no to purchases and spends a large percentage of her earnings on non-essentials. Hanah's spending habits are a stress on her marriage. Hanah's primary Money Role is Reckless.

Choose two Money Habits

Changing your Money Habits is an essential part of changing your Money Role. Let's start by determining your dominant Money Habits. As you read through the list of Money Habit examples below, think about the things you do with money when you're in your routine. They may or may not be compulsive habits, but they're definitely a well established and a familiar part of your behavior.

You have more than one Money Habit. Choose two habits you think are most related to the money situation you wish to improve (See what you wrote under *My Focus*). Write them down in the space provided in your *Logbook* under *My Two Money Habits*. Your habit may not be in the list of examples. That's okay.

Money Habit examples

- You spend to feel good, to celebrate, or to deal with boredom
- You buy what you can't afford or don't need
- You hide/lie about purchases
- You offer advice on and monitor other people's Money Habits
- You unnecessarily restrict your own spending
- You give money to people you think have poor Money Habits
- You undercharge for your services
- You spend most of your time working
- You borrow or take money from others
- You don't keep track of purchases
- You neglect your job
- You pay for more than your share of major expenses
- You do all the financial management for your family

- You almost never treat others by paying or picking up the check
- You buy things for status or to feel accepted
- You obsess about financial decisions
- You don't purchase necessities for yourself but are generous with others
- You spend without considering future needs
- You ignore good financial opportunities
- You let others make money decisions for you
- You find financial planning overwhelming and avoid it
- You pass up social engagements so that you don't have to spend money
- You're always the person who "picks up the check"
- You spend money to solve a relationship problem

Money Plain & Simple: Three Simple Steps

When you get right down to it, we interact with money in three basic ways:
- Habits
- Decision Making
- Planning

Money Plain & Simple will help you tackle each of these areas by following the **Three Simple Steps.**

Step One

3 Smart Habits a Day

Do three Smart Habits each day

1 You can do them when and where you like. You can make up as many new Smart Habits as you wish or stick to the same few. Your job is to create Smart Habits that work for your life. Now make a list of Smart Habits that can replace your two dominant Money Habits. Write your list of Smart Habits in your *Logbook* under My Smart Habit List. You can make additions and changes to the list whenever you like.

2 Next, choose three Smart Habits from your list that you will do the next day. We recommend you use your My Smart Habit List everyday to help you organize and plan your Smart Habits.

Before you get going, take a moment to give your Smart Habits a value. (See the Money Plain and Simple Smart Plan Chart in your *Logbook*.) You find out how the value of your Smart Habits works in *Step 3*.

3 Smart Dollars

At the end of each week, take the total number of times you performed your Smart Habits (see your *Logbook* and look at the Money Plain & Simple Smart Plan Chart) and pay yourself Smart Dollars. Your Smart Dollars are your Smart Habits converted to a dollar amount you will choose. These Smart Dollars provide the capital you will use for your Smart Plan *(Step 3)*. All you need to do now is to choose the value of your Smart Habits in dollars. The chart below gives examples of how different Smart Habit Values add up over time.

You can assign any value you like for your Smart Habits—from a penny to a thousand dollars, it's up to you. It's your money and you'll always have access to it in case of emergency. So if you choose a value that later seems too high or too low, simply adjust your Smart Habit Value as you go. You may prefer to accumulate your Smart Dollars in a no-fee bank account, a piggy bank or a cookie jar.

Habits are Powerful

Working with your habits is a key part of managing your Money Role. Habits are powerful forces in our lives. They have a profound effect on the way we feel and the way we see ourselves. Money situations are everywhere, that's where Smart Habits come in. Smart Habits will change the way you act and the way you see your Money Role. By adding just three new Smart Habits to your day you change the heart of your money problems. In time, your Money Habits will become a less dominant part of your life and your Smart Habits will become a lasting part of your improved Money Role. When you change your Money Role, you change your life.

Prepare

Prepare your Smart Habits. For instance, if you decide to take a lunch to work instead of eating out, make sure you have food in the fridge, pack your lunch the night before and figure out what you will say to your friends when they try to entice you into going to a restaurant.

Think

Pause and think about what you are doing when you do your three Smart Habits. Think about how these new Smart Habits prove that you can do more than your Money Role. When you stop and think as you are doing Smart Habits, you become more aware of your behavior. Your new awareness is a launching pad from which your Money Role evolves.

SMART HABIT VALUE IN SMART DOLLARS	MAX DAILY (3)	MAX WEEKLY (21)	MAX MONTHLY	MAX 6 MONTHS	MAX YEARLY
50¢	$1.50	$10.50	$42	$252	$504
$1	$3	$21	$84	$504	$1008
$3	$9	$63	$252	$1512	$3024
$5	$15	$105	$420	$2520	$5040
$10	$30	$210	$840	$5040	$10080

KEEP IT REAL

Scott's Money Habit is always saying yes to his kids when they ask for cash. If Scott decides to say no to every new request he wouldn't follow through because he still wants to be generous sometimes. It's okay to create an aggressive Smart Habit, but be realistic and choose something you are motivated to do. For Scott, a doable Smart Habit is deciding to say no to the requests he considers frivolous.

SMART HABITS ARE YOUR DECISION

You need to create your own Smart Habits; ones appropriate and personalized to your own way of doing things. For example, Monica who is Reckless stops buying coffee everyday. Monica's Smart Habit may not seem significant, but for Monica forgoing the daily coffee purchase is a significant choice that helps her change her Money Role.

BEWARE OF YOUR TRIGGERS

There are circumstances and relationships that will make you angry, annoyed, stressed and excited, triggering your old Money Habits. These triggers can be family, work, social events, stress, holidays, friends, moving and deadlines. When you get triggered the best strategy is to have a Smart Habit on hand.

A Smart Habit has two qualities:

1

It's different from the Money Habit you're trying to replace. It may or may not be the opposite behavior, but it supports the change you're trying to make. It's a different behavior that shouldn't leave you worse off than when you started. Here are two examples, one right, one wrong:

Do this:
Your Money Habit is avoiding bills. Your Smart Habit is to open bills as soon as they arrive, read them carefully, and attach them to the fridge with a magnet until they are paid.

Not that:
Your Money Habit is avoiding bills. Your Smart Habit is to file your unopened bills and avoid the filing cabinet.

2

Your Money Habits make you feel good. Therefore, your Smart Habits must be really rewarding and appealing so they can compete with your Money Habits and eventually become a permanent part of your life. Be honest with yourself. Don't choose a behavior that will make you feel unhappy, bored or deprived.

Do this:
Your Money Habit is maxing out your credit card by using it like it's cash-in-hand. Your Smart Habit is to leave your credit card at home and use cash or debit for purchases. You set aside an affordable amount of money each month for splurging on a purchase you enjoy.

Not that:
Your Money Habit is maxing out your credit card by using it like it's cash-in-hand. Your Smart Habit is to apply for additional credit cards so you have options when your card is declined.

Money Habits strengthen our Money Role and keep us in a financial rut.

Smart Habits help us change and meet our financial goals.

My day:

Reckless

	Gave kids money for lunch	Stopped for coffee and muffin before work
Ordered chinese for dinner	Ordered a new laptop	Went for pizza with Mike for lunch
Gave daughter money for a movie	Took son shopping after dinner	Bought a new case for my cell phone
Lied to wife when she asked if I had paid phone bill	Made plans with my brother to go to ski show this friday	Stuck unopened bills in filing cabinet

Smart Habit Examples

Profile	Money Habits	Smart Habit Examples
Situation: **Business Partner** **Money Role:** **Uncertain** **Goal:** **Wants to exit business partnership**	• Depends on others for advice • Always waits to see what her business partner will do • Doubts her desire to leave whenever her business partner assures her things are going well	• Creates a list of the reasons she wants to leave the business and reviews them once a day. • Determines how much money she needs to leave the business and creates a realistic budget, which she adheres to daily • Provides her partner with a timeline for leaving and begins a daily job search
Situation: **Single, no kids** **Money Role:** **Reckless** **Goal:** **Pay off debt and buy a condo**	• He spends money to network and meet the right people • Incurs debt to pay for courses, workshops, clothing, car and a career coach	• Nurtures and makes use of his current connections, friends and co-workers for advice and possible career connections • Restricts spending on training and appearance, and sets up a realistic, weekly debt repayment schedule • Schedules time to leverage free online resources and training, and enrolls in courses offered at work
Situation: **Parent, three children in university, hates job** **Money Role:** **Martyr** **Goal:** **Retire early**	• Urges his kids to give up their "dreams" and find stable, well paying careers like he did • Works long hours because he's worried he may be downsized • Stays at the same job he hates for 25 years because he is afraid to leave	• Stops advising his children and begins listening and supporting what they want out of life • Takes time to regularly update his resume and sets aside 15 minutes each day to search job postings • Analyzes his own skills and schedules time online and at the library researching the possibility of going into business for himself
Situation: **Sales VP** **Money Role:** **Deal Chaser** **Goal:** **Make a lot of money**	• Focuses on departmental results and ignores the developmental needs of her employees • Loses focus thinking about new or different opportunities • Whenever her team begins to encounter problems she finds a new position at a different company	• Meets regularly with employees to gauge morale and give feedback • Regularly seeks out and records feedback on her own performance from her boss, peers and direct reports • Stops checking the want ads and does one thing every day to improve the morale or performance of her department

Profile	Money Habits	Smart Habit Examples
Situation: **Works for family business** **Money Role:** **Unfulfilled** **Goal:** **Go back to school and become a physical therapist**	• Spends money on himself, his kids and relatives to feel better • Takes his kids out to eat when he is stressed • Complains about work	• Takes kids to the park and library • Schedules time for a walk after work to relieve stress • Donates time and help to relatives, rather than money or material goods
Situation: **Works for a landscaping company** **Money Role:** **Underachiever** **Goal:** **Wants to start his own landscaping business**	• Works long hours • Talks a lot about not having enough money to do anything he wants • Plays video games in his spare time	• Starts putting small amounts of money aside for a business • Starts taking small landscaping jobs on the side of his regular work to build a clientele • Looks into small business loans
Situation: **Married, works and has two kids** **Money Role:** **Penny Pincher** **Goal:** **Wants to stop fighting about money with her husband**	• Has husband pay for most expenses • Questions husband about his purchases • Fights with parents about how she and her husband spend money • Won't spend money on recreation	• Stops asking husband for money and uses her own money for purchases • Stops discussing purchases with parents and husband • Takes a vacation with husband
Situation: **Lives with sisters** **Money Role:** **Pious** **Goal:** **Wants to find a better job and move out on her own**	• Shares cooking and shopping with sisters to save money • Works at a job below her skill level • Rarely buys anything new for herself	• Goes out to lunch or dinner twice a week to talk with co-workers and make job contacts • Posts her resume on job boards as part of a job search • Buys a new outfit for a job interview

Step Two

Smart Decisions

In this step you'll learn how to make the right choices when facing high-stress money decisions.

Your Smart Decision Formula

Your Smart Decision Formula is simple: S.T.E.P. Stop, Think, Evolve, Persist. Your bottom line: when it comes to money decisions, don't let your Money Role dominate.

1 Stop

Don't make a snap money decision under high stress. Impulsive decisions are often mistakes and are always dominated by your Money Role instincts. Stop and take a step back from the situation.

2 Think

Think about your primary Money Role. What would you normally do in this situation? What are you feeling compelled to do in this moment? When you stop and think, you become much more aware of your behavior.

3 Evolve

Evolve your Money Role. Now that you've thought about what you'd normally have done, ask yourself what action you can take to resist your typical Money Role response. What can you do to put yourself on a new and different course? Make a Smart Choice that's outside the comfort zone of your old Money Role.

4 Persist

People encounter resistance when they make stronger choices. Stand by your Smart Decisions when you encounter resistance. Your Smart Decision might make you feel uncomfortable, or even alone. That's expected, it means you're making the right choice, so stick with it.

Relationships are major sources of stress and confusion in money decisions. These decisions aren't necessarily difficult because they involve a lot of money. Imagine you have a family member who's Reckless and is always borrowing money. They only ask for a few dollars, but they do it often, and it makes you irritated. Any emotionally loaded financial decision brings out the tension between your Money Role and your common sense. For example, Pamela knows she shouldn't give her brother a loan because he always defaults. However, as a Martyr, Pamela feels compelled to give her brother the money.

FAMILY DYNAMICS: RESISTANCE, SABOTAGE AND WELL-INTENTIONED DISTRACTIONS

Expect to encounter resistance, sabotage, and, distractions such as coaching and advice. Anticipate these dynamics and have a plan.

Your family and friends will typically:
- Try to help you with the program. You don't need help; Money Plain & Simple is designed to be a personal program. If they continue trying to be helpful, find a more private time and place to do your program.
- Tell you your changes are strange, unnecessary or negative. People are used to your old Money Role, so it will take them some time to get used to your new, improved Money Role and they'll complain until they realize your changes are here to stay.
- Tell you you're not doing your job, or living up to your responsibilities. For example, if you've always been a Martyr, some folks are going to feel that you're no longer doing your job by supporting their poor Money Habits—remember, that isn't your job, and it never was.
- Invent a crisis. A manufactured emergency is one way that people can compete for your attention or try to bring out your old Money Role. Don't fall for it. Keep using your Three Steps.
- Tell you they feel abandoned. For example, if you've always been a Deal Chaser and your best friend is a Deal Chaser too, they're going to feel left behind. You're not leaving them behind, you're just leaving them to Deal Chase on their own.

(See Logbook section Plan for Handling Difficult People.)

FAMILY MONEY ROLE PATTERNS

Every family has a few Money Roles that are part of their family life. The Munro's have a pattern of Reckless, which means shopping as recreation is a common family activity. However, only a few members of the Munro family have a Primary Money Role of Reckless, while many other members list Reckless as a minor role.

LOOK BELOW THE SURFACE

Our impressions of people's Money Roles are often wrong. For example, Alex who is an Underachiever, appears to be a confident, go-getter at work. However, Alex knows that his work attitude is an act he puts on to make up for his lack of confidence.

SMART HABITS ARE DIFFERENT FOR EVERYONE

When it comes to Smart Habits what works for you won't necessarily work for others. As an Underachiever, Joan's Smart Habit is to participate more at department meetings. Other Underachievers may not see the logic behind Joan's Smart Habit. However, Joan understands how her chosen Smart Habit helps her change her Money Role.

Smart Decision Examples

Dilemma	Smart Decision Formula
Unfulfilled Your sister-in-law asks you to help her launch her business	• **Stop:** Don't make a decision when there is pressure to do so. You tell your sister-in-law that you need a day to respond to her request. • **Think:** You want to say yes. As an Unfulfilled your instinct is to help your sister-in-law. You like 'helping' because it makes you feel vital, which is something that is missing from your job. As an Unfulfilled your pattern is to help others rather than addressing your own professional and personal development. • **Evolve:** You tell your sister-in-law that you are working on career changes and you are happy to listen and support her as she launches her business but you need to spend time on your own career. • **Persist:** Your sister-in-law responds by saying that she is very disappointed. You tell her that saying no is very difficult but doing well professionally is important to you. Now you feel guilty and worried. You reconsider your decision. You enjoy spending time with your sister-in-law. You think about how much your sister-in-law needs and would benefit from your help. You also believe that not helping family is selfish. You remind yourself that getting involved in your sister-in-law's project will hinder your own professional needs and your professional life is something that cannot continue to sacrifice. You stick to your decision and offer to help your sister-in-law find someone else to help with her business plans. You remind yourself that you are always generous and helpful with your family and this will not change.
Reckless Your father invites you on a vacation and offers to pay for your trip.	• **Stop:** Don't make a decision when there is pressure to do so. You tell your father that you will call him the next day with an answer and you thank him for his offer. • **Think:** Your instinct is to thank your parents and pack your bags. As a Reckless you usually say yes to gifts from family. You don't usually have money available for vacations. You are used to taking money from family and it's a common family practice. • **Evolve:** If you can afford to pay for the vacation and you want to go on the trip go but pay your own way. Make sure paying for the vacation won't require accumulating debt. If you cannot afford to pay decline. • **Persist:** Your parents tell you that you deserve a vacation. Thank them for their generosity but continue to refuse. Don't discuss the issue or get into any arguments about your decision. After you turn down the vacation you feel unhappy and deprived. You resist the temptation to spend money as a way to feel better. You remind yourself that being less Reckless with money will provide you with financial stability, less stress and more self-respect.
Martyr After almost 40 years of work you are planning on retiring but now you are reconsidering so you can help your son, who has recently lost his job.	• **Stop:** Don't make a decision when there is pressure to do so. You don't tell anyone at work or at home that you are reconsidering retirement. • **Think:** As a Martyr you have a strong urge to put off retirement to help your son with money. Your first instinct is to phone your son and tell him you will help him with money and that he should not feel stressed because you will give him money to pay his household expenses. • **Evolve:** You decide to stick to your retirement plan. You allow yourself the thought that you can always pick up some part time work if your son comes to you and asks for money. You also decide to help out by offering to watch your grandkids when your son goes on job interviews. • **Persist:** You continue to have thoughts of postponing retirement. You have major concerns and guilt about leaving your job when a member of your family is financially vulnerable. You remind yourself that you have always been a generous and supportive parent and your feelings are not logical but emotionally based. • You consider the idea that you always overcame financial challenges and that you should allow your son the opportunity to prevail during tough times. You remind yourself that you have always been and will always be there for your son, but helping him means letting him determine what he needs from you. You consider the fact that your son is a lot more resourceful than you are always willing to recognize.

Dilemma	Smart Decision Formula
Underachiever A new management position at work has opened up. You have the experience and interest.	• **Stop:** Don't make a decision when there is pressure to do so. Commit to following up on the opportunity. Put a sticky note on your computer monitor reminding yourself to apply for the job by the end of the following day. • **Think:** As an Underachiever you only apply for jobs if you are encouraged by the person offering the job or if you don't have a job. New positions and professional opportunities are always intimidating. Thus, your instincts are to file the job posting in a desk drawer and forget about it. As an underachiever you usually tell yourself that you need to focus on keeping your current job and pursuing a better one is irresponsible. You also put off moving forward in your career by telling yourself that you probably don't have the necessary experience or skills. • **Evolve:** Instead of avoiding your potential you ask your manager about the job opportunity. She says you are qualified and you respond by telling her that you will submit an application. That evening you update your resume and cover letter. • **Persist:** You applied for the job and now you are feeling vulnerable, uneasy and concerned that you made a mistake. You remind yourself that you always feel this way whenever you do something that challenges your lack of self-confidence. You remind yourself that whenever you have gone after an opportunity you have benefited.
Penny Pincher Shopping for your father's birthday you see something your father would really like but it is twice what you were planning to pay	• **Stop:** Don't make a decision when there is pressure to do so. Don't leave and walk away from the gift you are considering thereby making it impossible to buy. • **Think:** As a Penny Pincher your instincts tell you that the gift is too expensive and you want to leave the store. You start to come up with reasons against the purchase: 1. Your father doesn't care about gifts 2. Your father is also a Penny Pincher and will be shocked by an expensive gift. 3. You father won't bother to use the gift. You consider calling your sisters and asking them to buy the gift with you. • **Evolve:** You buy the gift because you realize that if you considered buying an expensive gift for your father it is something you can afford and it is something that your father will like. You figure your father can always return the gift if he doesn't like it but he should be the one to make the decision. • **Persist:** While waiting in line to pay for the gift you repeatedly think you are being too generous and you consider leaving without the gift. After you buy the gift you think about returning it. You also start looking for excuses to return it. You reconsider its merits and you try to convince yourself that your father won't really like it. You wrap the gift making it difficult to return and you bring it over to your sister's house where everyone will be gathering for your father's birthday party. You remind yourself that your incessant worrying and critiquing, has nothing to do with the gift and is what you typically do whenever you spend money. You also remind yourself that you always feel good when you give someone a thoughtful gift.

Smart Decision Examples (cont'd)

Dilemma	Smart Decision Formula
Deal Chaser You are almost finished putting together your new product line when you have an idea to improve your product. Your idea will take an additional 10 thousand dollars and 4 months.	• **Stop:** Don't make a decision when there is pressure to do so. Write out your idea for the new improvement but don't make a move either way. • **Think:** As a Deal Chaser your instincts tell you that the product will be much better with the improvements and the sales will be higher. You want to put off finishing the product and add the new changes, spending additional money and time. You also want to start telling people about the proposed changes to try to recruit them to the new plan. Thinking about the changes makes you feel excited because you feel like the changes will bring you major financial success. You want to stop production on the current product and figure out how to meet your new goals. • **Evolve:** You remind yourself that although you think these changes seem really great, your pattern is not completing projects so you decide to finish the product without adding the additional changes. You tell yourself that these changes can always be made during the next manufacturing cycle when various changes will have to be made to upgrade the technology. • **Persist:** Having made the decision to not make the changes you feel deflated and down. You continue to revisit your decision. You stick to the task of seeing the product through its manufacturing process and focus on marketing and sales. Eventually you begin to feel good when you see the product selling.
Pious You are looking for a business partner. One of your friends offers to introduce you to someone who is looking for a business partner. The prospective partner is wealthy.	• **Stop:** Don't make a decision when there is pressure to do so. You tell your friend you need a few hours to think it over. • **Think:** As a Pious your instincts tell you that you will have nothing in common with a wealthy person and you will only be able to relate and connect on a superficial level. You want to say no to your friend's offer. You think going into business with a rich person will only lead to conflict over money. • **Evolve:** After hearing more about the prospective partner and determining that he has the necessary business experience you agree to a meeting. • **Persist:** As the day of the meeting approaches you feel certain that it will go badly and you consider canceling. You remind yourself that you have misjudged people and situations in the past and your assumptions about the meeting are typical of how you think and act around rich people. Your meeting goes well and you make plans to get together again. Afterwards you begin to worry that you won't get along with a rich person but you focus on making decisions that are best for the business.
Uncertain You are setting up your own business. A former co-worker comes to you and proposes that you form a business together.	• **Stop:** Don't make a decision when there is pressure to do so. You tell your co-worker that you will get back to him in a few days. • **Think:** As an Uncertain your instincts tell you to go into business with your co-worker and you want to say yes to the offer. Despite your skills, experience and connections you continually underestimate and undervalue your abilities. When it involves financial opportunity you always pick the most cautious option regardless of its shortcomings ignoring their liabilities and effectively restricting your financial growth. • **Evolve:** You decide to strike out on your own because it's what you have always wanted. You call your co-worker and tell him your decision. You suggest meeting once in a while to discuss business. You think if you need help you can call a former co-worker. You remind yourself that you can always bring in a partner at a later date but doing so now out of a fear of failure is a bad choice. • **Persist:** You continue to revisit the decision and wonder if you didn't make a mistake by turning down the partnership. A few of your family and friends question your decision. You let their remarks sit without explaining because you feel clear about your choice. By the end of the week you wonder how you gave the partnership serious consideration when you have always wanted to work by yourself.

Master your financial goals and change the way you see money for life.

Step Three

Smart Planning

So far you have learned how you can simply and successfully change your habits and decisions to improve your relationship with money and achieve future financial goals. That leaves Money Planning.

Your task in Step Three is to build a Smart Plan. A Smart Plan helps you achieve the Focus in Question One in *Getting Started*.

1 First look at your Focus in *Getting Started*. Do your answers still ring true? Revise your Focus if you wish and write it in the *Money Plain & Simple Plan* section in your *Logbook*.

2 Your Money Plain & Simple Plan is made up of Three Strategies. Read through the list of strategy examples. Choose or create three personalized strategies that will help you achieve your Money Plain & Simple Focus. Make sure your Strategies are the opposite of your typical Money Role choices and inclinations. Write your strategies in the *Money Plain & Simple Plan* section in your *Logbook*.

3 Next, decide when to access your Smart Dollars and how much money to apply to each strategy. Write your decisions in the *Money Plain & Simple Plan* section in your *Logbook*. For example, you can invest your Smart Dollars by spending them on a vacation, or by saving them in a savings account/piggy bank. Money Plain & Simple is flexible—make it work for you. Use the *Money Plain & Simple Smart Plan Chart* to organize and track your progress.

Once you have achieved your Focus, you can set a new Focus, create new Strategies and build a new Smart Plan.

For more examples visit
www.moneyplainandsimple.com

Realizing financial security and success is now more convenient with the new Money Plain & Simple iPhone App. Track and plan your progress on the go. Find the App at moneyplainandsimple.com or iTunes.

Smart Planning Strategies

Three Simple Steps

Strategy	Requires Smart Dollars	Possible Money Roles Affected
Negotiate a manageable debt repayment program with a CCCS planner	$	Reckless, Deal Chaser, Martyr, Uncertain, Pious
Obtain a low-interest consolidation loan to repay high interest credit card debt	$	Reckless, Deal Chaser, Martyr, Uncertain, Pious
Invest in your 401k (RRSP)	$	Penny Pincher, Reckless, Deal Chaser, Martyr, Uncertain, Pious
Build your credit rating by getting a secured credit card in your own name		Reckless, Uncertain
Sell your luxury and non-essential items		Reckless
Separate your bank accounts from your spouse		Martyr, Reckless, Uncertain, Deal Chaser
Stop paying other peoples bills		Martyr
Start your own business	$	Uncertain, Deal Chaser, Pious
Learn to take care of your own bills and financial planning	$	Uncertain, Pious, Martyr
Purchase a second home or invest in real-estate	$	Penny Pincher, Pious, Martyr
Invest in a life-insurance policy	$	Penny Pincher, Pious, Uncertain
Start an education savings plan for your child	$	Penny Pincher, Pious, Uncertain, Reckless, Deal Chaser
Begin monthly contributions to index mutual funds or GIC	$	Penny Pincher, Pious, Uncertain, Reckless, Deal Chaser
Retain a career coach or head hunter to evaluate your resume and skill sets	$	Underachiever, Penny Pincher, Pious, Uncertain, Deal Chaser
Take classes or training to advance your career and open doors	$	Underachiever, Penny Pincher, Pious, Uncertain, Deal Chaser
Secure a job	$	Deal Chaser, Pious, Uncertain, Underachiever
Pay back taxes	$	Reckless, Deal Chaser, Martyr, Uncertain, Pious
Stop using credit cards	$	Reckless, Deal Chaser, Martyr
Set strict limits to helping others with money or advice, and stick to them		Martyr
Take a vacation and buy non-essentials for yourself	$	Martyr, Underachiever, Penny Pincher

Plan
change
transform

Money Plain & Simple Levels of Change

As you use Money Plain & Simple, you can expect to experience three levels of change. Knowing about these levels will help you set realistic expectations and timelines for achieving your Focus. Take the time you need to achieve your Focus. Money Plain & Simple is designed to be like a comfortable hike, not a sprint.

Level One: Plan

What this level is about
- defining your Focus
- discovering your Money Role and Money Habits
- choosing Smart Habits
- creating a Money Plain & Simple Plan
- beginning to use your Smart Decisions Formula

What you can expect to happen
The first level of Money Plain & Simple lasts about two weeks, but can take a longer or shorter time. Becoming aware of your Money Role and Money Habits is a critical change all on its own. During this level, expect to learn new things about yourself and your relationship with money. For the first time, you're becoming fully aware of your Money Role and Money Habits, and seeing them in action.

What to watch out for
You may feel like an observer, watching yourself act out your Money Role and Money Habits, but unable to stop or control them. This is perfectly natural.

You may be tempted to try to completely change your primary Money Role.
For example, if you discover you're Reckless you may decide you want to become a Penny Pincher. Don't work against yourself. Trying to swap one Money Role for another will drain you of energy and make you frustrated. Your Money Role is a fundamental part of who you are. As you progress through these levels, you'll learn to work with it.

What to keep in mind
Be patient, because during the next level you'll learn to interact with your Money Role in new ways. Eventually the tables will turn. The point of this first level is awareness. Then, by working with your habits, decisions and plans, you'll learn to make your Money Role work for you and take control of your financial life.

Level 1 – **Rachel is a Deal Chaser**

"My husband and I fight about money all the time. If we could just figure out the money we might have a chance at saving our marriage."

Rachel has a business degree and works at a large hardware store. She's married and owns a small house she inherited from her parents. Her husband works installing digital hardware systems for a telecommunications company. Rachel likes to travel and shop. She has a small business selling antiques and collectables over the internet. Rachel and her husband have no savings and have twice mortgaged their home. They cannot afford a health insurance plan to help pay for her husband's diabetes and asthma treatments. Rachel and her husband fight about money all the time. Her husband feels like Rachel should not be spending their money on her business ventures. They have been separated twice.

Rachel's financial ruts

Over the last twelve years Rachel has started seven new businesses and switched jobs five times. She has worked as an EMT and a jewelry designer. She sold real- estate, had a salon and now works in a hardware store. Rachel tends to ignore her paid work job to work on start-up ventures. Currently she spends all her free time and some of her work time trying to resell things she buys at estate sales over the internet. She has spent all her savings on these purchases and her husband has given her money to help. Rachel has not stayed at any one job for more than a year.

Rachel's Money Plain & Simple Action Plan

Focus on her paid work. Stop spending money on new ventures. Be more honest with her husband about her financial situation.

Rachel decides to forgo making any more purchases for her internet collectables business until she can sell all her present inventory. She meets with her manager at the hardware store to discuss her performance and look at what she can do to move up in the company. She commits to not starting a new business venture for at least three years.

Rachel's Money Role changes
"I'm beginning to take my job at the hardware store more seriously. I want to do well there and maybe work towards managing one of the bigger stores in the area. I also see how all the jobs and business ventures have created a lot of unnecessary stress and sacrifice for myself and my husband. I have stopped lying to him about how my business ventures are doing. I think I can be happy if I have some savings and a secure job. But I still think about changing jobs and trying something new. It's a struggle because although now I can see how my deal chasing has been bad, still almost every day I see something that I want to explore. But I guess that if I'm meant to do something else I will figure it out eventually and it won't mean sacrificing money or well-being to do it."

Rachel's biggest challenge
"I've always had a project or start-up business to make me feel excited and now I have to find something else to feel excited about."

Rachel's big insight
"I can't believe how many businesses I've started over the years. It seems a bit crazy."

Level Two: Change

What this level is about
- learning more about your Money Role
- using Smart Habits that work well
- dealing with disruptions and resistance
- getting better at using your Smart Decisions Formula

What you can expect to happen
The second level can last between three to six months, but this is only a guideline. It's important to take as much time as you need.

During this level, expect to start seeing connections between the relationships you have with your family and friends, and your relationship with money. You may also start to see the Money Roles of those around you. You'll begin to understand how your Money Role has influenced your life choices and led to your current financial situation. During this level it's natural to want to refine your Focus and your Money Plain & Simple Plan. Feel free to do so.

What to watch out for
Don't expect to make major changes immediately. In fact, don't be surprised if at times you feel confused, alone, anxious, or frustrated. You may even feel like giving up. Don't. Money Plain & Simple isn't a race. Take your time, follow the Three Simple Steps and stick to your Plan. Success is going to happen when you least expect it.

Expect to encounter resistance.
You're starting to use your Smart Decisions Formula.

Smart Decisions can be one of the most challenging aspects of Money Plain & Simple. You're changing your routine, and this may be uncomfortable for you and for others. Expect some resistance. Be patient and don't give in to self-doubt. Don't be tempted to argue with others or try to please them.

What to keep in mind
When it comes to progress, cut yourself some slack. It's natural to start evaluating your progress at this point. Put aside any preconceived notions you may have of where you think you should be. Concentrate on your Smart Habits and Smart Dollars. Stick to your Money Plain & Simple Plan, and use your Smart Decisions Formula. Achieving your Focus is what matters, not how fast you get there.

If you feel you're not progressing as quickly as you'd like, ask yourself these questions:

1. Do you enjoy doing your Smart Habits?
2. Do your Smart Habits help to reduce stress in your day?
3. Are you doing your Smart Habits for yourself and not to make someone else happy?
4. Does your Focus excite you? Will it improve your life?

If you answered "no" to any of the questions, you should review your Smart Habits and develop some new ones. You're the only one who knows what you want to change, and how and when to change it.

Celebrate the small steps. Your long-term goal may be one of considerable change, but you get there by acknowledging and appreciating the small accomplishments you make along the way. Paying down a mortgage doesn't happen in a day.

Level 2 – **Ryan is a Penny Pincher**

"I'm tired of working with family. I want to go back to school or get a job I like.""

Ryan is 32. He has been working for his family's landscaping business since high school. He also works part-time with his sister in her real-estate business. He claims that the family businesses are poorly run and will fail if he leaves. Ryan constantly worries about what he considers his family's "unnecessary spending".

Ryan's financial ruts
Ryan spends most time trying to manage his family's spending habits. Ryan does all the banking, payroll and taxes for both businesses.

Every few years Ryan talks seriously about leaving the business and spends some time looking into the possibility of starting a business of his own or going back to school. But he always chooses to stay where he is. He likes the steady paycheck and he worries about spending money to go back to school or start his own business.

Ryan's Money Plain & Simple Action Plan
Spend some money on career changes. Share financial responsibilities. Try to tone down criticisms of other's spending.

Ryan decides to share the accounting duties with his parents and siblings. He lets his sister and mother help with the banking, and he accepts his younger brother's offer to take over payroll.

Ryan decides that he will leave the family business and gives himself a year and a half to make the transition. He also commits to taking two classes at a local college. He is working on cutting back on his negative comments about his family's spending habits.

Ryan's Money Role changes
"I've begun to realize that I can't control the money decisions in my family and the family businesses. I spend lots of time trying to stop my family from what I think is frivolous spending, without thinking about the cost to me. I have stopped habitually second-guessing everyone's decisions at work, which is hard because I worry that my parents and brothers waste money.

I am clear that not spending money on school is holding me back and is actually costing me money, not saving it. The money I spent on tuition this semester was well worth it".

Ryan's biggest challenge
"My big challenge is just spending money. Being cheap is like a bad habit that I don't entirely want to give up."

Ryan's big insight
"I am now clear that I need to get a life outside the family business, and that being cheap is keeping me from living my life. The more I let my Money Role dominate my spending habits, the less happy I am. So being unhappy and being cheap seem to go together for me".

Level Three: Transform

What this level is about

- attaining your Focus
- maintaining your changes and setting a new Focus
- continuing to learn more about your Money Role, Money Habits and Smart Decisions, andmaking changes that help you get ahead

What you can expect to happen

This third and final level of progress has no timeline. Money Plain & Simple permanently transforms the way you view your relationship with money. It sheds light on your financial relationships with others. There's no turning back from your new self-awareness.

During this level you can expect to achieve your Focus. Your Smart Habits are easier to accomplish, and some may even feel like second nature. You have a new sense of power and confidence. You know a Smart Decision when you make one and are much more comfortable with the Smart Decisions Formula. You're maintaining the changes you've made in levels one and two because they've helped you reach your goal.

What to watch out for

Some of your friends and family members still resist your new routines, but you've learned to accept this.

What to keep in mind

Money Plain & Simple is a tool for life.

It's time to set new goals, create some new Smart Habits and build a new Plan. There are no limits to what you can achieve using Money Plain & Simple.

Level 3 – **Mike is a Martyr**

> "I want to retire or at least cut down to part-time hours but I don't think my kids will be able to survive without my financial support."

Mike is 64 years old. He is an independent contractor and a professional electrician. Mike has been working since he was 18 and has always given his mother money. He gives his brothers money and helped put his youngest brother through college. He is married and has two grown kids and three grandkids. His wife is a nurse. Mike and his wife would like to retire. They are concerned about their kids who are struggling to pay bills. Mike thinks that if he retires he won't be able to continue helping his kids out financially. Mike is also supporting his mother who is in a nursing home.

Mike's financial ruts

Mike has a difficult time asking his brothers to help pay for their mother's nursing home bills. When Mike hears that his sister-in-law has lost her job he offers to give her money without waiting to hear if she needs help.

Mike's Money Plain & Simple Action

PlanGive less money and advice to others. Work less. Ask for help. Share financial responsibilities.

Mike has stopped taking work projects that extend more than six months. He has made plans with his wife to spend part of the winter vacationing in South Carolina. Last week he had breakfast with his brothers and asked them to help more with their mother. Mike has also started to ask his kids how they are doing instead of automatically offering them money. Mike asks his youngest son to help him clean and repair the family camping site.

Mike has sat down with his wife and a financial planner from their bank to talk about a retirement plan.

Mike's Money Role changes

"I still spend a lot of time worried about my kids and what they will do without my financial help. But now I also think about myself and what my needs are. I also try to ask how people are doing rather than just offer money. It's really hard being a father and a brother and not doing my usual habit of helping with advice and money."

Mike's biggest challenge

"I feel guilty when I see my son and don't give him money. My big challenge is maintaining my sense of being a good man without giving money."

Mike's big insight

"I can finally see how my Money Role has dominated my outlook. I'm starting to wonder why I keep worrying about other people and why I think everyone I know needs money and advice."

Join us at moneyplainandsimple.com for more information about how to accomplish your financial goals.

The website is also a great place for more information about Money Roles, and additional solutions and strategies to money challenges.

Connect to moneyplainandsimple.com for answers to problems like:

1
My brother and I grew up in the same house with the same parents. Why is my brother a Deal Chaser, while I am an Unfulfilled?

2
How do I get my sister to stop asking me for money?

3
How can I use the Money Plain & Simple program to save my marriage?

Go to moneyplainandsimple.com and download Money Plain & Simple IPhone app. Create and track your Focus, Smart Habits, Smart Decisions and chart your Money Plain & Simple progress.

Logbook

This is your Logbook and there is no right way to use it.

I recommend using it to track your Focus. You can also maintain a record of your Smart Habits and Smart Dollars. You can note the Smart Habits and Decisions that work well. You can keep track of triggers and relationship changes and organize strategies for handling difficult situations.

The Logbook can be a journal for understanding your Money Role and its connection to your financial choices.

Three Easy Rules for Success with the Money Plain & Simple Logbook

1: Record daily
For best results, use your Logbook everyday to record your Smart Habits and keep track of your Smart Dollars.

2: Use it
Reading and writing about challenges, successes, triggers and people will help you stay connected and on course with your goals.

3: Take it with you
I recommend carrying your Logbook with you. I pull it out and flip it open when I am feeling overwhelmed or when I have a new insight about my relationship with money. The tips and strategies keep me from doing too many old Money Habits and it's convenient for logging my Smart Habits and Smart Dollars. Reading and writing in it underscores my progress which keeps me motivated.

My Focus

Choose an aspect of your life that involves money, and needs to change and write it down here.
It may involve a personal relationship, employment, your unfulfilled potential or your family life.

Focus: _____

Now imagine it's the future, you've used Money Plain & Simple to achieve your Focus. List one or two things in your life that have now improved.

Scott's Focus: I need a good job with a good salary.

Scott's future Improvements: I have health insurance and I can afford to take a trip

Improvements: _____

_____

_____

_____

_____

_____

_____

_____

Money Plain & Simple is a tool for life. Once you've reached the objectives you're setting now, you can continue to use the program to set a new Focus.

Money Roles

A Money Role describes your basic feelings and responsesto money. Money Roles are shaped by your upbringing, family and major life experiences, but when you get right down to it, they're made up of emotions. A Money Role comes from the feelings of comfort, fear and concern you've learned to associate with money. Your Money Role is behind every financial decision you make and exercises a great deal of control over your life, easily overriding your own best interests and commitments without you realizing. Money Roles are a natural part of life; everybody has one.

Ask yourself: which of the Money Roles (see Getting Started) best describes who I am when I am making everyday choices? Most people are a mix of one primary Money Role and two or more minor Money Roles.

My Money Roles (I am sometimes these Money Roles): _____

_____

My Primary Money Role: _____

_____

_____

My Two Money Habits:

As you read through the list of Money Habit examples (see Getting Started) think about the things you do with money when you are in your routine. Your Money Habits are familiar to you and they can appear during emotional highs and lows. You will have more than one Money Habit. Choose two habits.

_____

_____

_____

_____

My Smart Habit List:

Smart Habits I can use instead of my two most dominant Money Habits

1. _____
2. _____
3. _____
4. _____
5. _____
6. _____
7. _____
8. _____
9. _____
10. _____

11. _____
12. _____
13. _____
14. _____
15. _____
16. _____
17. _____
18. _____
19. _____
20. _____

Instructions for Money Plain & Simple Smart Plan Chart

Each day enter the number of Smart Habits you have completed under its day of the week column. At the end of the week add up the total number of Smart Habits the week. Then enter the total in the column, Total Weekly Smart Habits.

Now, take your total from that week and multiply it by the Smart Habit Value you have assigned for that week. (Keep in mind you can change your SmartHabit Value anytime you wish).

Enter the result in the Total Smart Dollars for the Week. Use the column Running Total for my Smart Dollars to keep track of your running total.

Money Plain & Simple Smart Plan Chart

Number of Smart Habits

week #	Mon.	Tue.	Wed.	Thu.	Fri.	Sat.	Sun.
1							
2							
3							
4							
5							
6							
7							
8							
9							
10							
11							
12							
13							
14							
15							
16							
17							
18							
19							
20							
21							
22							
23							
24							
25							
26							

Total weekly	Smart Habit Value	Total Smart Dollars for the week	Running total my Smart Dollars

Money Plain & Simple Plan Chart (cont'd)

week #	Mon.	Tue.	Wed.	Thu.	Fri.	Sat.	Sun.
Number of Smart Habits							
27							
28							
29							
30							
31							
32							
33							
34							
35							
36							
37							
38							
39							
40							
41							
42							
43							
44							
45							
46							
47							
48							
49							
50							
51							
52							

Total weekly	Smart Habit Value	Total Smart Dollars for the week	Running total my Smart Dollars

My Money Plain & Simple Plan

Focus: Improvements:

_____   _____

_____   _____

_____   _____

_____   _____

_____   _____

Strategies* * Your strategies must be uncharacteristic of your Money Role and Money Habits	Smart Dollar amount	Money will be used on this date	Notes
_____	_____	_____	_____
_____	_____	_____	_____
_____	_____	_____	_____
_____	_____	_____	_____
_____	_____	_____	_____
_____	_____	_____	_____
_____	_____	_____	_____
_____	_____	_____	_____
_____	_____	_____	_____

My Potential Pitfalls

Note three things you could imagine yourself potentially doing that would prevent you from achieving your Money Plain & Simple Plan:

1. _____

2. _____

3. _____

Tracking Smart Decisions

Use this chart to track and examine your experiences with Smart Decisions. Making Smart Decisions takes practice. Most people see significant improvements by their second or third decision.

How to read the chart:

Decision – What was the decision about?

Circumstance – Who was involved?
When and where did the decision come up?

My Concerns – What were your immediate concerns or thoughts?

My Response – What did you say and do?

Smart Formula – What happened when you tried the Smart Decision's formula?

Reactions – How did people respond when you didn't make a decision that was typical of your Money Role?

Discovery – What did you learn about your Money Role?

Smart Decisions Chart

Decision	Circumstances	Concerns

Response	Smart Formula	Reactions	Discovery

My Triggers

There are circumstances and people that will make you angry, annoyed, stressed or excited and trigger your Money Habits: family, work, social events, stress, holidays, friends, moving, deadlines. These are your triggers, and they will drain your drive and resolve. Many of us make the mistake of believing that we can simply ignore, avoid or rise above our triggers. This strategy pretty much never works. If you want to succeed be realistic, accept that you will get triggered and have a plan and a Smart Habit to handle the moment.

Triggers – circumstances and people:

Strategies:

_____   _____

_____   _____

_____   _____

_____   _____

_____   _____

_____   _____

_____   _____

My Plan For Handling Difficult People

Your family and friends are familiar with your old Money Role, so it will take them some time to get used to your new, improved Money Role they'll complain, try to compete for your attention or try to bring out your old Money Role until they realize your changes are here to stay. The best way to manage difficulties is to anticipate the events, people and reactions involved and stick with your Smart Habits and Smart Decision Formula.

These questions help you identify any potential challenges and how to effectively respond to them.

1. A person who plays a major role in your life.

_____

2. A past conflict or stressful issue involving the two of you.

_____

3. How did this person respond to the conflict/issue?
What did they say and do?
(example: give advice, ask for advice, cry, shout, get violent, make threats, withdraw, pretend nothing happened, invent a crisis, complain that you have changed, tell you that you are being irresponsible, complain that you are not being fair or kind)

_____

_____

_____

4. How do they behave when you have tried to make changes in the past?

_____

_____

5. How do you usually respond to their demands?

_____

_____

6. How do you sabotage yourself when you are trying to make changes?

_____

_____

My Financial Life Events

List five major financial life events/decisions.
Beside each explain how it relates to your Money Role.

1. _____

_____

2. _____

_____

3. _____

_____

4. _____

_____

5. _____

_____

For more information about the topic or if you would like to do more work on your Financial Life Events see www.moneyplainandsimple.com

My Family Money Mapping

Remember: Money Roles are shaped by our upbringing, family and major life experiences. Therefore family can be helpful in understanding how we think about and what we do with money. Your answers to these questions will help you recognize the key factors influencing your past and current relationship with money.

1. Your mother's Money Role. _____

_____

_____

2. Your father's Money Role. _____

_____

_____

3. Your partner's Money Role. _____

_____

_____

4. Your siblings' Money Roles. _____

_____

_____

5. Do you know your grandparents' Money Roles. _____

_____

_____

6. Influence your parents' and siblings' Money Role had on your life

_____

_____

_____

7. How your Money Role has impacted your family.

_____

_____

_____

8. Your parents' financial expectations for you when you were growing up.

_____

_____

_____

9. Your mother/father/partner's weakness with money. _____

_____

_____

10. Your mother/father/partner's strength with money. _____

_____

_____

*To figure out your family's Money Roles look at people's behavior instead of what they say they do or intend to do. For example, while Allyson says she is strict and unyielding about giving money to her kids, she always gives into her sons' requests for loans.

For more information about the topic or if you would like to do more work on your Financial Life Events see www.moneyplainandsimple.com

Find your Money Role Partner

We often seek partners who help us play-out our Money Roles. For example, a Reckless will find a partner who will be responsible for all financial decisions. Penny Pinchers feel useful when they are cautioning their family and friends against over-spending. It's helpful to understand how the major relationships in your life influence your Money Role.

It's important to note that no one type of Money Role partnership is better or healthier than another. The key to doing well and meeting your money potential is managing your Money Role. And managing your Money Role is your job.

1. Uncertain and Penny Pincher
2. Uncertain and Martyr
3. Uncertain and Pious
4. Pious and Unfulfilled
5. Deal Chaser and Martyr
6. Deal Chaser and Penny Pincher
7. Deal Chaser and Underachiever
8. Reckless and Penny Pincher
9. Reckless and Martyr
10. Pious and Underachiever
11. Unfulfilled and Penny Pincher
12. Unfulfilled and Martyr

Money Role Test

Your Money Role is the key to achieving your financial potential. Once you know your Money Role you can immediately start making changes by managing your Money Role's influence on your life. These scenarios will help you figure out your Money Role.

Scenario 1: A family member asks you for money

1. What is your answer, yes or no?
2. What are your immediate instincts?
3. What are your concerns?
4. If you decide to help, what role will you play?

Scenario 2: A trusted friend and former colleague phones to offer you a job interview. The position is your ideal job and offers opportunity for advancement.

1. What do you do and say?
2. What are your immediate instincts?
3. What are your concerns?
4. If you decide to say yes, what role will you play?

Now look at your answers to the scenarios.
Compare your answers to the Money Role descriptions. You should find one primary Money Role that links all of your responses together. You will also find your answers relate to two or more minor Money Roles.
If you cannot find connections between your answers and the Money Roles, you may need a few days to get some perspective about your Money Role.

Money Plain & Simple offers hands-on seminars, personalized consulting, and assessments for your business and management needs. Sessions are simple to follow, practical and interactive with engaging scenarios and support material. Here are some of seminar topics:

- Principles of Money Plain & Simple
- Identifying and managing your Money Role
- Performance Improvement, Turnaround and Restructuring Services
- High stakes financial decision making
- Hiring and leadership
- Money and family business
- Dynamics and longevity
- Financial restructuring and crisis
- Recovery and renewal
- Businesses on the fault line
- Finding financial confidence and vision
- Community and non-profit organizations: vision, values and money without compromise